The Reproductive System

Injury, Illness and Health

Steve Parker

Heinemann Library
Chicago, Illinois

Originated by Ambassador Litho
Printed and bound in China by South China Printing Company

07 06 05 04 03
10 9 8 7 6 5 4 3 2 1

Library of Congress Cataloging-in-Publication Data
Parker, Steve.
    The reproductive system / Steve Parker.
        v. cm. -- (Body focus)
Includes bibliographical references and index.
Contents: Reproduction -- Frmale reproductive organs -- Female cycle -- Egg cells -- Female menstrual problems -- Other female problems -- Male reproductive organs -- Sperm cells -- Male problems -- Reproductive infection -- Reproductive health -- Sperm and egg -- Embryo and fetus -- Childbirth -- Indancy and childhood -- Adolescence and puberty -- Fertility problems -- Fertility control -- Assisted reproduction -- Reproduction and genetics.
    ISBN 1-4034-0199-3 (lib. bdg. : hardcover) --ISBN 1-4034-0455-0 (pbk.)
    1. Human reproduction--Juvenile literature. 2. Generative organs--Juvenile literature. [1. Reproduction.] I. Title. II. Series.
    QP251.5 .P37 2002
    612.6--dc21

                                        2002014431

Acknowledgements
The publishers would like to thank the following for permission to reproduce photographs:
p. 4 Corbis Stock Market/Tom & Dee Ann McCarthy; p. 5 Corbis/Jennie Woodcock; p. 7 Science Photo Library/Simon Fraser; p. 10 Science Photo Library/Professors P. M. Motta & J. Van Blerkom; p. 12 Science Photo Library/Laurent, Yakou; p. 14 Science Photo Library/Dr. E. Walker; p. 15 Science Photo Library/Keith, Custom Medical Stock Photo; pp. 17, 20 Science Photo Library; p. 19 Science Photo Library/Professor S. Cinti, CNRI; p. 21 Science Photo Library/Gary Carlson; p. 22 Science Photo Library/CNRI; p. 24 Telegraph Colour Library/David McGlynn; p. 25 Corbis Stock Market/Pete Saloutos; p. 26 Science Photo Library/K. H. Kjeldsen; p. 27 Science Photo Library/D. Phillips; p. 28 Science Photo Library/Pascal Goetgheluck; p. 29 Science Photo Library/Hank Morgan; p. 30 Corbis/Jules Perrier; p. 31 Corbis/Jon Spaull; p. 33 Corbis Stock Market/Ariel Skelley; p. 34 Corbis Stock Market/Jon Feingersh; p. 35 Corbis Stock Market; p. 37 Science Photo Library/Oscar Burriel; p. 39 Science Photo Library/Adam Hart Davis; p. 40 Stone/Getty/James Darell; p. 41 Science Photo Library/James King Holmes; p. 42 Corbis; p. 43 Corbis Stock Market/George Shelley.

Cover photograph of a colored X-ray showing the human female torso, with an artwork representation of the reproductive organs, reproduced with permission of Science Photo Library.

The publishers would like to thank David Wright for his assistance with the preparation of this book.

Every effort has been made to contact copyright holders of any material reproduced in this book. Any omissions will be rectified in subsequent printings if notice is given to the publishers.

Some words are shown in bold, **like this.** You can find out what they mean by looking in the glossary.

CONTENTS

# REPRODUCTION

The word *reproduction* means "making or producing more of the same kind." It is a feature of life itself. All living things reproduce to make more of their kind. All the parts of the body involved in making new individuals are known collectively as the reproductive system.

The basic process of reproduction in humans, and the body parts involved, are much the same as in other animals. In particular, they are very similar to those of other mammals—warm-blooded animals with fur or hair who feed their babies milk. In almost all mammals, the baby develops inside the female's body, in a specialized part called the womb, or **uterus.** The baby leaves the womb during a process known as birth. After birth, the baby is fed milk made by the mother.

Female and male

There are two kinds or sexes of human beings—female and male. Each has a different role in reproduction. In fact, the major differences between the female human body and the male human body are in the reproductive parts themselves. Other differences are influenced by the way the reproductive parts work and the products they make, such as **hormones.**

Reproduction makes not only more human beings, but also parents, children, and families.

The reproductive system is the only system in the body that changes considerably after birth. Its parts are present during childhood, but they are not fully developed or able to function. They usually develop to their mature, working condition during the early teenage years, although there is great individual variation. The process of change in the structure and function of the reproductive system and the time when it occurs are known as **puberty.**

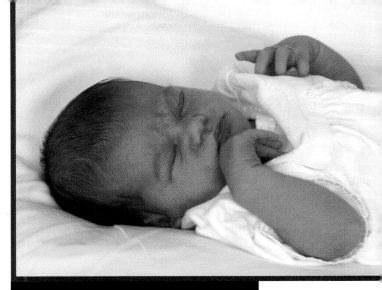

The day of birth may seem like day one, but babies begin to develop nine months earlier.

The developing baby

All parts of the human body consist of microscopic **cells.** The female reproductive parts make special cells called **egg** cells. The male reproductive parts make microscopic cells called **sperm** cells. For reproduction, a sperm cell is transferred to the female body—during **sexual intercourse**—and joins with an egg cell. This joining is known as **fertilization.** The result is a fertilized egg called a zygote, which is smaller than the head of a pin.

The fertilized egg grows and develops for nine months inside the uterus of the female. This time is known as pregnancy, or **gestation.** During the earliest stages of development, until about eight weeks after fertilization, the new individual is known medically as an **embryo.** From about eight weeks after fertilization until birth, it is known as a **fetus.** During this time the new life is recognizably human. In everyday terms, however, the developing individual before birth, and afterward, is usually called the baby.

Views and attitudes
Sexual reproduction and the growth of a baby in the uterus are entirely natural processes. However, attitudes toward them vary hugely around the world. People have vastly different views about how and when sex should occur and whether or not a woman and man who produce a child should be married.

These views and attitudes vary among people of different cultures, traditions, ethnic groups, social backgrounds, and faiths. Although reproduction is a basic biological process, some people feel awkward or embarrassed when discussing sexual matters or problems of the reproductive system.

# FEMALE REPRODUCTIVE ORGANS

The main parts of the female reproductive system are in the lower **abdomen** of the body. They consist of the **ovaries**, the **fallopian tubes** or oviducts, the **uterus**, and the **vagina**.

Ovaries

The two ovaries are the main female reproductive parts, and they are positioned on either side of the lower abdomen. They produce the **egg cells** and retain them until each one ripens and is released. The ovaries also make natural body chemicals called **hormones**, which control the female cycle of fertility—the times when it is possible to begin or **conceive** a baby, and the times when it is not.

Each ovary is about half the size of a hen's egg. The inner structure of the ovary, and how the egg cells develop inside it, are shown on the following pages.

Medicine and reproduction

The workings of the reproductive system can be altered by many kinds of medical procedures and modern technologies. This is true of both the female and male reproductive systems. Often the aim is not to treat a health problem but to make it possible for an individual to become a parent or prevent the conception of a baby.

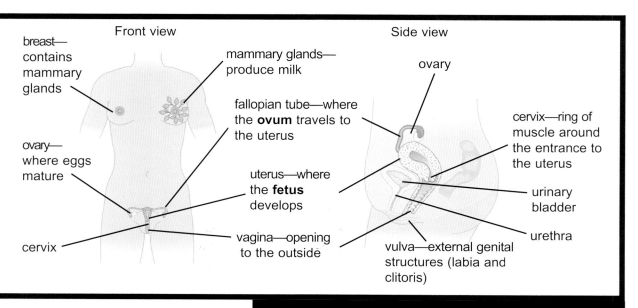

Front view

breast—contains mammary glands

mammary glands—produce milk

fallopian tube—where the **ovum** travels to the uterus

ovary—where eggs mature

uterus—where the **fetus** develops

cervix

vagina—opening to the outside

Side view

ovary

cervix—ring of muscle around the entrance to the uterus

urinary bladder

urethra

vulva—external genital structures (labia and clitoris)

This diagram shows the female reproductive organs.

Fallopian tubes

Each of the two fallopian tubes links an ovary with the uterus. The tube is about four inches (ten centimeters) long and carries a ripened egg from the ovary to the uterus. Near the ovary, the fallopian tube widens into a funnel shape and has a fingerlike edge. This ends wraps around part of the ovary. The other end of the fallopian tube opens into the uterus.

Uterus

The uterus is a pear-shaped organ at the base of the lower abdomen. Its thinner end points down and back, and its thicker end tilts up and forward, above the **bladder.** The uterus is, in effect, a container with very thick, muscular walls. The space inside the uterus is usually very small and squashed almost flat. However, during pregnancy the uterus enlarges as the baby develops inside. In a woman who has not had children, the whole uterus is slightly smaller than her clenched fist. After bearing children, it is usually larger.

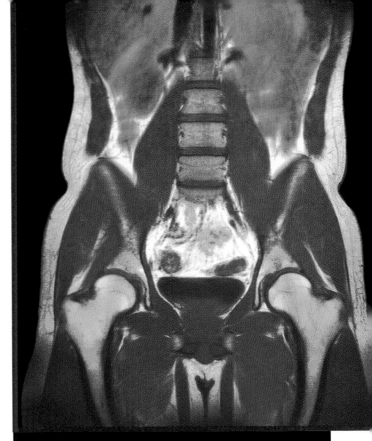

This ultrasound scan shows the female reproductive parts.

Vagina

The lower, narrow end of the uterus is called the neck or **cervix.** It opens into the vagina, also known as the birth canal. The vagina opens to the external genital parts, or the vulva, between the legs. During birth, the baby leaves the uterus and passes through the vagina to reach the outside world.

Mammary glands

A newborn human baby usually feeds on milk made by its mother's two **mammary glands.** These glands are within the breasts. The milk they produce has precisely the right amount of **nutrients,** including sugars, fats, **proteins,** vitamins, and minerals, for the new baby. The mammary glands are generally regarded as part of the female reproductive system. Not all babies breastfeed. Babies can thrive on nonhuman milk, including special formula milks.

FEMALE CYCLE

A woman cannot **conceive** a baby at just any time. The female reproductive system works in a rhythmic fashion called the **menstrual cycle.** A typical cycle lasts about 28 days and then begins again. It is possible to conceive a baby only during a few days within each cycle.

Ripening of the egg

During the first part of each cycle, an **egg cell** in one of the **ovaries** becomes mature, or ripe. The egg develops within its tiny container or capsule, known as the **follicle.** In a typical menstrual cycle, the ripening of the egg begins at day 1 or 2 and continues for the next 12 to 13 days.

Release of the egg

From about day 5 to day 6 of the cycle, the inner lining of the uterus starts to become thick with **nutrients** and blood-rich tissues. This makes the lining, known as the **endometrium,** able to receive and nourish a fertilized egg so that it can begin to develop into a baby.

On day 14 of a typical cycle, the ripe egg is released from its follicle. This process is known as **ovulation.** The ripe egg passes into the funnel-shaped end of the **fallopian tube** and moves along the tube to the **uterus.** If **fertilization** of the egg by a **sperm** is to occur, it most likely will happen during the egg's journey along the fallopian tube.

Control of the menstrual cycle

Natural body chemicals called **hormones** control the female menstrual cycle. There are four main hormones involved:

- FSH, or follicle-stimulating hormone, is released by the **pituitary gland** just below the brain. It stimulates an egg to ripen in the first part of the cycle.
- **Estrogen** is produced by the ripening follicle and causes thickening of the uterine lining.
- LH, or luteinizing hormone, is also released by the pituitary gland. It causes the follicle to release its egg and then change into another structure, known as the corpus luteum.
- Progesterone is produced by the corpus luteum, which also makes some estrogen. These two hormones maintain the thickened uterine lining until the cycle ends.

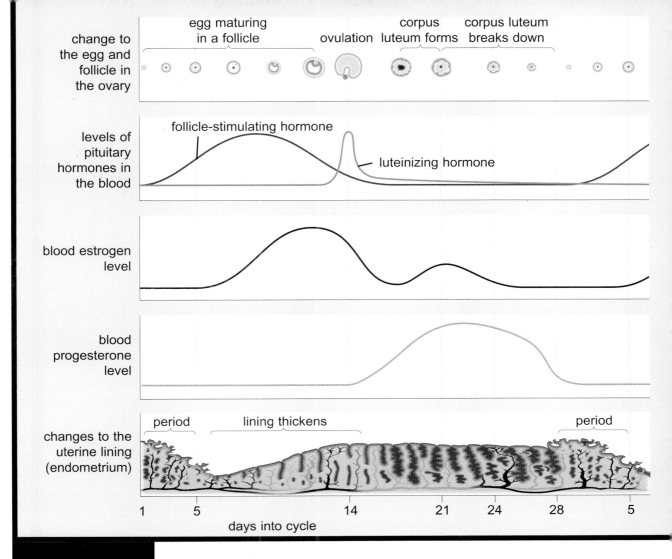

change to the egg and follicle in the ovary

egg maturing in a follicle · ovulation · corpus luteum forms · corpus luteum breaks down

levels of pituitary hormones in the blood

follicle-stimulating hormone

luteinizing hormone

blood estrogen level

blood progesterone level

changes to the uterine lining (endometrium)

period · lining thickens · period

days into cycle: 1 5 14 21 24 28 5

A lot of changes, including hormone levels, occur during the menstrual cycle, which lasts roughly 28 days.

No fertilization

If there is no fertilized egg, the thickened lining of the uterus begins to break down toward the end of the cycle, usually from day 24. The blood and tissues are lost through the **vagina** as the menstrual flow or period. The beginning of this loss marks the end of one cycle, at day 28, and the start of a new one, at day 1 again. A period usually lasts 3 to 5 days.

PMS

Premenstrual syndrome, or PMS, usually occurs in the few days before a period starts. There are often changes in mood, feelings, and emotions, along with changes in the physical body, such as enlarged and tender breasts, a bloated feeling in the stomach, and swollen ankles. The changes in hormone levels can also result in feelings of being nervous and "on edge."

PRODUCTION OF EGG CELLS

A typical ripe **egg cell,** also called an **ovum,** is incredibly tiny. However, compared to other cells in the body, it is relatively huge. It is far larger than the equivalent male cell, the **sperm.**

Formation of egg cells

When a baby girl is born, she has about 300,000 unripe egg cells in each **ovary.** Many of these gradually break up, or disintegrate, during childhood. By the time of **puberty,** there are about 150,000 eggs. On average, during the years when a woman has her menstrual cycle—between approximately 15 and 50 years of age—about 400 to 500 eggs will ripen and be released. Usually one egg is released in each **menstrual cycle,** from alternate ovaries.

A ripe egg cell is released from its follicle. It floats into the fluid inside the fallopian tube. This is called ovulation.

The ripening follicle

At the start of the menstrual cycle, during days 1 to 5, several egg cells are stimulated to ripen, and their **follicles** enlarge. By day 6, one of these has become dominant and continues its development, while the others shrink away. The dominant follicle becomes larger, and the cells forming its outer layers produce the **hormone estrogen.** A **nutrient**-rich fluid collects inside the follicle, nourishing the egg cell as it passes through its final stages of ripening.

Ovulation

The fully ripe follicle, called a Graafian follicle, is about 0.12 inch (2 millimeters) across. On or around day 14 of the cycle, the follicle explodes and propels the ripe, mature egg cell into the nearby funnel-shaped end of the **fallopian tube.** The egg cell is now ready to be **fertilized** by a sperm cell. The explosive release of the egg cell from the follicle is called **ovulation.**

Multiple births

In most cases, only one baby at a time develops in the **uterus.** In other cases there are multiple babies—twins, triplets, and so on. For nonidentical, or fraternal, twins, two eggs are released from the ovary at about the same time. Each egg is fertilized by a sperm and develops from the beginning as a separate individual. The twins are as similar as ordinary brothers or sisters, but they are not identical. For identical twins, the two individuals come from the same fertilized egg, so they have exactly the same **genes.** Identical twins are always the same sex—either both girls or both boys—and they look very similar.

Cell division—mitosis and meiosis

Each cell in the human body contains **genetic** material, or genes, in the form of a substance called **DNA.** Genes are the instructions for how the body develops, grows, and carries out life processes. Each body cell has two complete sets of genes. One came originally from the mother, and one came from the father. Genes are packaged into tiny, threadlike structures called **chromosomes** inside the cell. There are two sets of 23 chromosomes, for 46 total chromosomes.

New body cells are formed by the division, or splitting, of cells. Cell division occurs to add extra cells during growth, to repair injured parts, and to replace old, worn-out cells as part of regular body maintenance. Ordinary body cells divide by a process called **mitosis.** During mitosis, both sets of genes are copied.

Egg and sperm cells are produced by a different type of cell division, called **meiosis.** The original cell divides to form four resulting cells, instead of two. Also, the genes are halved to one set of 23 chromosomes in each egg or sperm. Then, when egg and sperm join, the double set is restored.

MENSTRUAL PROBLEMS

The timing of the **menstrual cycle** and the length of its different stages may vary greatly—both among individual women and within the same woman over time or with changing circumstances. Most women come to know their own cycle and how their bodies work and feel during their cycle. Changes should be reported to a doctor, although usually there is no cause for concern when changes do occur.

Menstrual problems

Most problems with the menstrual cycle are due to changes caused by the **hormones** that control and coordinate the cycle. Dysmenorrhea involves discomfort or pain in the lower **abdomen** at or around the time of the period. It is often called menstrual cramps, and it may be due to spasm or contraction of the muscles in the **uterine** wall.

Menorrhagia is a heavier than normal menstrual flow or bleeding. It may or may not be accompanied by pain. Amenorrhea is when menstrual cycles and their periods cease altogether. It can be caused by ill health or weight loss due to another health problem. The symptoms of oligomenorrhea are infrequent or longer than usual cycles. Again, these symptoms may be due to another illness.

Around the time of their periods, women often experience pain or discomfort in the lower abdomen.

Menopause

Menstrual cycles are likely to be quite changeable and erratic when they first begin during **puberty.** Likewise, cycles become more variable in the year or two before **menopause,** usually around the age of 50 to 54 years. The changes in the cycle and the hormones during menopause can affect other parts of the body. Women may experience hot flashes or sweats, heart palpitations, joint pain, mood swings, headaches, and weak bones.

Effects of menopause

The female hormones that control the menstrual cycle can also affect other body systems and functions. One effect of menopause, which occurs in about 20 percent of women, is considerable weakening of the bones, which is called osteoporosis. In these cases, the bones become brittle and fragile. Osteoporosis may cause backaches, and the bones are more likely to break during a fall or similar accident.

A healthy diet and plenty of exercise during a woman's earlier years encourages strong bones. Also, strong bones can better withstand menopausal changes. Treatment with hormone-containing drugs, known as hormone replacement therapy (HRT), may help protect women against osteoporosis and ease other symptoms of menopause. However, recent studies have suggested that some forms of HRT may have harmful side effects.

Endometriosis

Sometimes small pieces or fragments of the uterine lining, or **endometrium,** become stuck along a fallopian tube or the lower body cavity. Instead of leaving the body, they remain stuck. Each month they become rich with blood and then break down, just as the rest of the lining does. This is known as endometriosis. However, the blood cannot escape, and it may irritate surrounding areas such as the intestines or **ovaries.** Symptoms include pain and extra amounts of bleeding during the period. Treatment may include HRT and perhaps surgery to remove the fragments.

Treatments

There are various underlying causes of menstrual problems, and some are described on the following pages. In other cases they are due to an imbalance of the hormones that control the menstrual cycle. There also may be no obvious physical cause. Modern medical treatments, such as pills or tablets that affect the hormonal cycle, are usually successful in reducing pain and other menstrual symptoms. The contraceptive pill can be especially useful for this.

Unlike other parts of the body, such as the heart or brain, most of the reproductive organs do not perform vital life processes, so they are not essential for survival. However, healthy behaviors and regular checkups are important to keeping them healthy. When a problem does occur, surgery and/or drugs are usually successful for treating them.

Ovarian problems

An ovarian cyst is a fluid-filled bag in the **ovary.** It may be small and painless, or it may grow larger and interfere with **hormone** production and the **menstrual cycle.** It can cause pain and press on the nearby **bladder.** The causes of ovarian cysts are unclear, although some result from abnormal ripening of an **egg** in its **follicle.**

Very rarely, an ovarian cyst may become malignant or cancerous. Again, the reasons for this change are not usually clear. The malignancy tends to cause vague symptoms in the early stages, such as discomfort in the lower **abdomen.** Later symptoms include weight loss and abdominal pain. Treatment may be a combination of surgery, radiation treatment, and anticancer drugs.

Cervical problems

In cervical dysplasia, the **cells** that form the **cervix** lining change, and there is an increased risk of further cancerous changes. What triggers these alterations is not clear, but cervical cancer is one of the most common cancers affecting women. It causes abnormal discharge and bleeding from the **vagina,** pain, and general ill health. Treatment may include a combination of surgery, radiation, and anticancer drugs. The surgery usually includes removal of the **uterus,** known as a hysterectomy, and perhaps the ovaries and other reproductive parts.

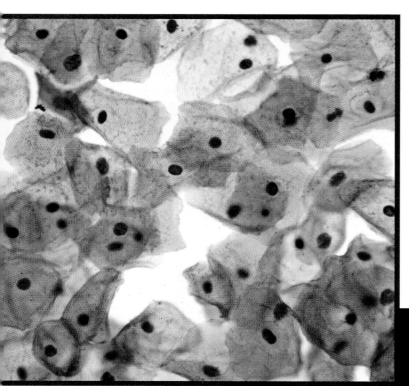

Cervical cells taken during a Pap smear test are studied under a microscope. These cells are healthy.

A less serious cause of symptoms similar to cancer of the cervix is a cervical polyp. A polyp is a bulging, grapelike growth of the lining. It can usually be surgically removed.

Uterine problems

Fibroids are benign, or noncancerous, growths in the muscular wall or on the surface of the uterus. In many cases they appear for no clear reason. Symptoms include heavy and painful periods and perhaps a hard lump in the lower abdomen. Small fibroids that do not cause problems may be monitored at checkups, but larger or troublesome ones are surgically removed.

Cancer of the uterus usually begins on the inside—in the lining, or **endometrium.** It may cause vaginal discharge, painful periods, and irregular bleeding or "spotting" between periods.

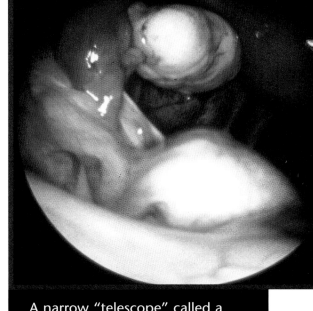

A narrow "telescope" called a laparoscope allows doctors to examine reproductive and other parts inside the abdomen. This view is of a healthy uterus, ovaries, and fallopian tubes.

In a uterine prolapse, the muscles and **ligaments** that normally hold the uterus in place become loose and slack. The uterus tends to sag and bulge downward into the vagina. This may happen after childbirth or with age.

Other conditions

In some cases the reproductive system develops abnormally. A retroverted uterus slopes up and rearward, rather than up and forward. In persistent cloaca, the opening of the vagina is shared with those from the urinary and digestive tracts. The symptoms of such conditions vary enormously. In some cases they may cause inability to have children. Surgery can often correct the defects.

Cervical smear (Pap) test

A common procedure at a woman's checkup is a cervical smear, or Pap smear, test. *Pap* is short for *Papanicolaou,* the name of the person who devised it. During a physical examination of the reproductive system, a small sample or smear of microscopic cells and fluid is taken from the cervix. It is then examined under a microscope. The test detects abnormal changes, which could signify early stages of cervical dysplasia or cancer.

In the male human body, the main parts of the reproductive system are in the lower **abdomen** and just below it. They consist of the **testes, scrotum, epididymides, vas deferens,** prostate gland, **seminal vesicles,** and penis.

Testes and scrotum

The two testes, or testicles, are contained in a bag of skin called the scrotum. The scrotum hangs below the lower front of the abdomen. The testes produce the male reproductive **cells,** or **sperm** cells. They also produce male sex **hormones.** The main male sex hormone is **testosterone.** It controls the production of sperm and the development of the male's body features, such as facial hair, muscle bulk, and deep voice. Each testis is about three-quarters of the size of a hen's egg.

Epididymides

Each of the two testes is connected to an epididymis, a tube about twenty feet (six meters) long. The epididymis is folded and coiled so much that it forms a mass only about two inches (four centimeters) long, draped over the top and side of the testis. The epididymis stores sperm cells after they have been produced in the testis but before they leave along the next part of the system, the vas deferens.

Vas deferens

Each vas deferens, or sperm duct, is a tube-shaped continuation of the epididymis. It is about eight inches (twenty centimeters) long. It curves upward into the abdomen and then inward and down behind the **bladder.** Here it joins the duct from another reproductive part—the

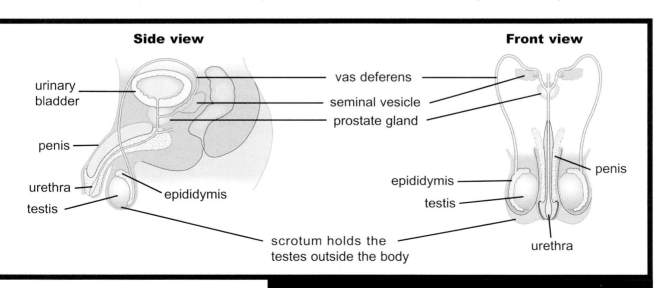

This diagram shows the male reproductive organs.

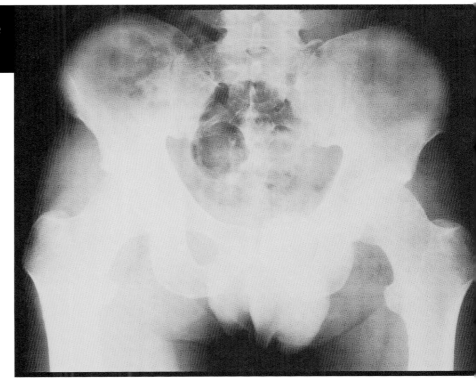

This colored X-ray shows the male reproductive parts.

seminal vesicle—to form the ejaculatory duct that carries sperm on their journey out of the body.

Seminal vesicles and the prostate

The two seminal vesicles are shaped like a pinky finger, but slightly smaller. They lie alongside the end parts of the vas deferens, behind the bladder. They make a fluid that provides sperm cells with **nutrients** and energy. The fluid passes out through a duct at the base of the seminal vesicle. Here, it joins the sperm in the vas deferens.

At the point where each vas deferens joins a seminal vesicle, it is called the ejaculatory duct. The two ejaculatory ducts pass through the prostate gland, behind and below the bladder. The prostate is about the size and shape of a chestnut. Like the seminal vesicles, it makes fluid to stimulate and help the sperm on their journey.

Penis

At the base of the prostate, the two ejaculatory ducts join yet another tube, the urethra. When sperm are released, they pass into the urethra, which runs along the inside of the penis. The penis is rod-shaped and lies just in front of the scrotum. The urethra ends as a small opening at the tip of the penis. This is where sperm leave the male reproductive system.

Two-purpose tube

The tube called the urethra has two main functions. During urination, it transports the waste liquid urine, which is made by the kidneys, from the bladder and out of the body. During **ejaculation**, it carries sperm in their fluid from the reproductive system and out of the body.

PRODUCTION OF SPERM CELLS

Like an **egg cell** in the female reproductive system, a **sperm** cell in the male reproductive system carries one-half of the **genetic** material needed to make a new human being. However, compared to the egg cell, the sperm cell is tiny. It is shaped like a tadpole, with a bulging head, rodlike body, and long, thin, flexible tail. Its total length is so tiny that 200 sperm cells placed end to end stretch less than half an inch (about one centimeter). Most of a sperm's length is its tail.

Making sperm cells

Like egg cells, sperm cells are made by a special type of cell division called **meiosis**. During meiosis, the genetic material is split in half. The female reproductive system works in a cycle of activity, with one egg ripening every 28 days. The male reproductive system works continuously. Sperm cells are being produced all the time, day and night, many thousands each second.

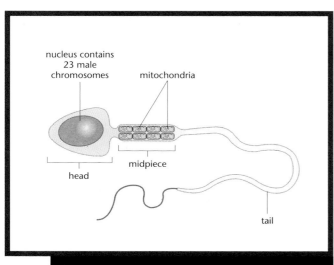

Each tiny sperm has three main parts: the head, the body, and the tail. All the vital chromosomes are stored in the head.

The process of making sperm cells is called spermatogenesis. It begins in the **testes** and ends in the **epididymides**. Each testis consists of about 800 tiny coiled tubes called seminiferous tubules. Straightened and joined together, the tubules from one testis would stretch more than 650 feet (200 meters).

Inside the testis

The inner lining of each tubule contains large rounded cells called spermatogonia. These divide continually to form more cells. As this happens, the cells change shape from round to tadpole-shaped. They also move from the lining around the inner edge of the tubule toward the space in the middle.

Sperm storage

The resulting spermatids move along their tubules, which join together and carry them into the epididymis. Here they finish their development and become fully mature. The whole process of maturation for a single sperm takes about two months. Each sperm can live for another month. They live in the epididymis or the first part of the **vas deferens**. Sperm that are not released during ejaculation break apart and disintegrate and are replaced by the continuing supply of new sperm cells.

Swimming abilities

Mature sperm thrash their long tails to swim toward the female egg cell. However, they need help in their long journey from the epididymis, along the vas deferens and urethra, out of the male body, into the **vagina** of the female, through the **cervix**, into the **uterus**, and along the **fallopian tube**, until they finally reach the egg cell. This help is provided by wavelike movements called **peristalsis** of the muscles in the various tubes and ducts along the route.

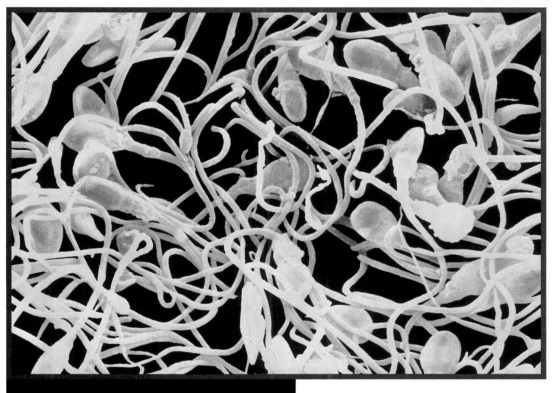

Some 300 to 500 million active sperm are released during ejaculation.

Sperm and fluid

The fluid that contains sperm cells is called semen, or seminal fluid. It is the combined product from the epididymides, **seminal vesicles**, prostate gland, and other glands. The total volume of fluid released during a typical ejaculation is about one-tenth of an ounce (3 to 4 milliliters). Only a tiny fraction of its volume is sperm cells, and yet there are 300 to 500 million of them. Having too few sperm cells, known as a low sperm count, may cause problems in **conceiving** a baby.

MALE REPRODUCTIVE SYSTEM PROBLEMS

Surgery and/or drugs are effective for the treatment of many problems of the male reproductive system. Treatments vary depending on whether or not the affected man wants to father children in the future. Some problems do not affect the function of the reproductive system, but they do cause pain or irritation that interferes with **sexual intercourse** and so with the ability to have children.

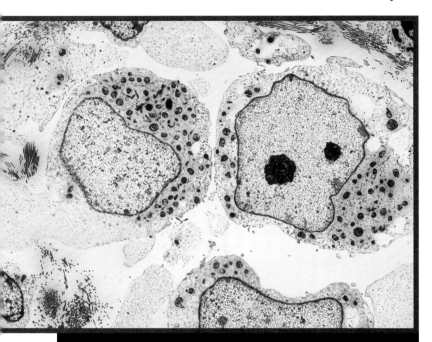

Small samples of cells from the testis, prostate, or other male parts are taken by a process called a biopsy. They are studied under a microscope to detect changes such as cancer. These rapidly dividing cancer cells are inside a testis.

Testicular problems

The two **testes** hang loosely in a skin pouch, the **scrotum**. In rare cases, a testis may twist out of position, putting a kink into its **blood vessels**. This is known as testicular torsion, and it causes pain and swelling. It often occurs for no clear reason. The testis may untwist naturally, but some cases need urgent medical treatment.

Hydrocele is a soft swelling around a testis, caused by an excess of the fluid that normally cushions and protects it within the scrotum. The condition is usually painless or slightly uncomfortable. The fluid can be removed, or its production lessened by a minor operation.

Cysts

Epididymal cysts are baglike pouches of the **epididymis** in which **sperm** and fluid gather. They usually form painless swellings on the upper or side portion of the testis. Treatment is not usually necessary unless they become uncomfortable.

Prostate problems

Several conditions can affect the prostate gland. Benign prostatic hypertrophy, or BPH, is an enlarged prostate. BPH is a noncancerous condition that often affects a man's ability to urinate, since the urethra, which carries urine, passes through the prostate and may be narrowed or pressed closed by the enlargement. Cancer of the prostate can cause similar symptoms. Prostate cancer is less likely to spread to other parts of the body than other cancers are. Sometimes prostate cancer is only

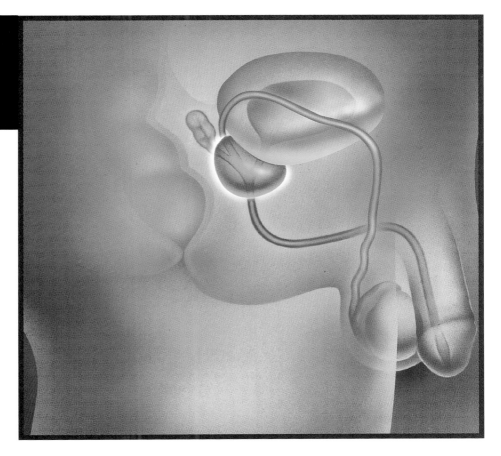

The prostate (blue, upper) wraps around the tubes carrying urine and sperm.

discovered at a checkup for other health problems. It often progresses slowly. Treatments include various forms of surgery and drugs.

Inguinal hernia

The inguinal canal is a tunnel-like gap through which the testes descend from the **abdomen** into the scrotum. The testes usually take this position before birth, and the canal is then pressed closed. An inguinal hernia is a weakness in the muscles of the groin that allows abdominal parts, such as the intestine, to protrude down the inguinal canal. It may appear as a bulge or dragging feeling in the groin. It needs medical assessment.

Testicular cancer

Testicular cancer is one of the most common forms of cancer in men, especially between the ages of 20 and 40 years. A growth appears as a lump in the affected testis. The cause is usually unclear. Early detection and treatment have a high success rate, which is one reason why regular checkups are vital. In particular, a weekly self-check of the testes is recommended, gently feeling for any changes or unusual swelling, lumps, discomfort, or pain.

REPRODUCTIVE INFECTIONS

Certain infections by harmful **microbes** affect the reproductive system directly. Early treatment with **antibiotics** is very effective in most cases of such infections. Some of these infections are called sexually transmitted diseases (STDs), as they are passed on as the result of various forms of sexual contact. Others are not transmitted sexually. Instead, they spread in other ways. Other infections, such as HIV/AIDS, may be passed on by sexual contact, but they affect other parts of the body and not the reproductive system.

Complications

Infections of the reproductive system may cause inflammation, scarring, and blockage of various parts. This can affect general health, the function of the closely connected urinary system, and the ability to have children. Also, a pregnant woman can pass some infections onto her baby in the **uterus** or during birth. In undetected cases, the baby is at serious risk of problems such as pneumonia, slow mental development, eye infection, or even blindness.

Chlamydia

Nongonococcal urethritis (NGU), or chlamydia, is caused by the microbe *Chlamydia trachomatis*. In women it can cause inflammation of the urethra, **cervix**, and **fallopian tubes**, as well as **vaginal** discharge. In men, the urethra, prostate, and **epididymides** are usually affected, with discharge from the penis and discomfort or pain. There also may be more widespread symptoms, such as lung and eye infections.

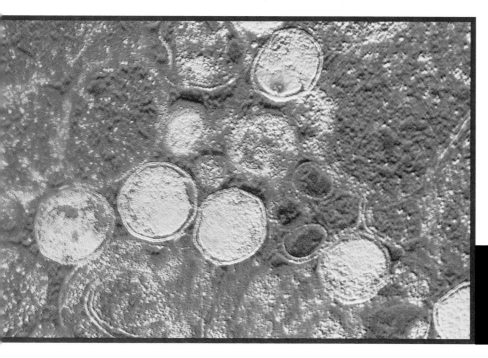

Powerful microscopes are used to look at the microbe that causes chlamydia.

Genital herpes

Also called type II herpes simplex, genital herpes is caused by the *Herpes simplex* **virus.** Herpes usually begins with itching, and then small, painful blisters appear on the genitals. Herpes is very contagious, and the blisters may spread. Over a few days these burst and crust over. Other symptoms include fever and swelling and pain in the groin area.

Gonorrhea

The **bacterium** *Neisseria gonorrheae* can affect the reproductive and urinary systems in women and men. Symptoms in both sexes range from mild discomfort to urethral discharge, itching, and burning pain. Men may have inflammation of the epididymides. Women may have a cervical discharge. A complication of gonorrhea is arthritis or painful joints. Gonorrhea is a leading cause of these problems in young adults.

Syphilis

Syphilis is a dangerous disease caused by the bacterium *Treponema pallidum*. It usually appears as a hard sore or ulcer, called a chancre, that forms where the bacterium entered the body, such as on the genitals. Other symptoms that appear sometime later include skin sores and rashes, pain, swollen glands, and fever. These may fade, but if not treated, syphilis can lead to paralysis, mental problems, and even death.

Pelvic inflammatory disease

Pelvic inflammatory disease (PID) is a general term for inflammation and infection of a woman's pelvic region—the lower **abdomen** including the reproductive and urinary parts. PID is a complication of several reproductive infections. It can affect the uterus, fallopian tubes, **ovaries,** and other organs. Consequences sometimes include the inability to have children.

Reducing risks

The risks of contracting a reproductive system infection, or a general infection that affects other parts of the body, are influenced by several factors. These include the number of sexual partners, the amount and type of sexual contacts, and the personal hygiene habits a person has. In particular, the spread of HIV/AIDS is greatly affected by sexual factors. At present, there is no cure for AIDS, and it is ultimately fatal. Use of a condom can significantly lower the risks of transmitting many types of STDs.

REPRODUCTIVE HEALTH

Like all parts of the body, the reproductive system benefits from good health habits. These include eating a balanced diet, getting plenty of exercise, getting sufficient rest and relaxation, and avoiding excess stress and harmful substances, especially certain drugs. There are also many ways to maintain reproductive health.

In addition to their use as a contraceptive, condoms help reduce the risk of passing on many types of sexually transmitted diseases.

Self-exams

Most doctors recommend that each person be aware of his or her own body. This includes doing regular checks of the reproductive system. During a self-examination, a person should check for lumps, soreness, pain, swelling, redness, discharge, and other unusual signs. Women should examine their breasts, men should examine their **testes**, and both should examine urinary and reproductive openings and the genitals.

Vital health checks

Health professionals also perform checkups, which include screenings such as the Pap smear test. The frequency of these varies with age, medical and family history, whether a woman has had children, and other factors.

Regular self-exams and checkups are vital. However, some people regard reproductive body parts—

Planning children

A woman planning to become pregnant can take various measures to safeguard her health and that of her baby. In particular, she can stop smoking (which is always helpful), stop or minimize alcohol use, and eat a nutritious, balanced diet. Both tobacco and alcohol, if consumed by a pregnant woman, are known to damage the baby's well-being.

even their own—as somehow different from other body parts. They may feel awkward or embarrassed about them. But many problems that affect the reproductive system can be treated much more easily and successfully if detected early.

A protective cup for the genital area is a vital piece of equipment in many sports.

Hygiene

The external genitals should be washed and cleaned thoroughly and regularly, as part of normal hygiene. Left unclean, the moist surfaces encourage **microbes** and infection. Uncircumcised boys and men should clean under their foreskin, the flap of skin around the front of the penis. Protection from the microbes that cause sexually transmitted diseases includes using a condom during **sexual intercourse.**

Accident and injury

Like any body part, the genitals and reproductive system are at risk of physical injury or trauma. This can occur when there is a blow to the lower **abdomen** or groin, or if the body's weight falls there. The male reproductive parts, being outside the abdomen, are especially at risk.

Apart from pain and damage, even if the injury heals, it can jeopardize a person's ability to have children in the future. So it is important to wear approved protective clothing and equipment, such as chest shields for girls and women and athletic supports and cups for boys and men.

The danger of drugs

Drugs such as steroids may be misused in pursuit of building muscles or gaining an advantage in sports. Some of these steroids "copy" the effects of sex **hormones** such as **testosterone.** They can have very harmful side effects, including damage to the reproductive system that can prevent a person from being able to have children.

SPERM AND EGG

The main event in normal reproduction is when the **nucleus** of an **egg cell** from the mother joins with the nucleus of a **sperm** cell from the father. Thus begins the development of a new individual. The joining of the nuclei of the two sex cells—egg and sperm—is known as **fertilization.**

Journey of the egg

The egg, or **ovum,** is released from the **ovary** at **ovulation.** Unlike sperm cells, which can swim by thrashing their tails, the egg cannot move under its own power. It passes from the ovary into the widened end of the **fallopian tube** and is then carried along toward the **uterus** by two processes. The first one is **peristalsis.** The other is the flexing of microscopic hairs, called cilia, that line the fallopian tubes. The cilia swish with a rowing motion similar to tiny oars.

These two actions create a slow flow of fluid in the fallopian tube, which carries the egg along. Even so, the egg's almost four-inch (ten-centimeter) journey to the uterus may take between four and seven days.

Journey of the sperm

Sperm cells have a much longer journey than the egg cell does. The journey begins in the male's **testes** and **epididymides,** then moves along the **vas deferens,** ejaculatory ducts, and the urethra in the penis. The release of many millions of sperm in their fluid from the male reproductive system is called ejaculation.

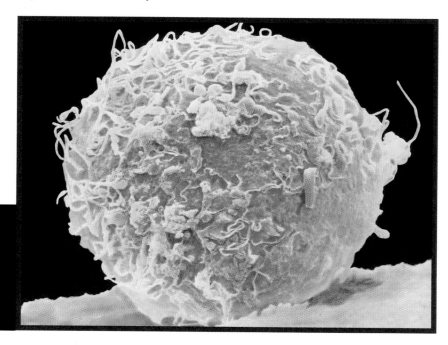

Many sperm gather around the huge egg, but only one joins with it.

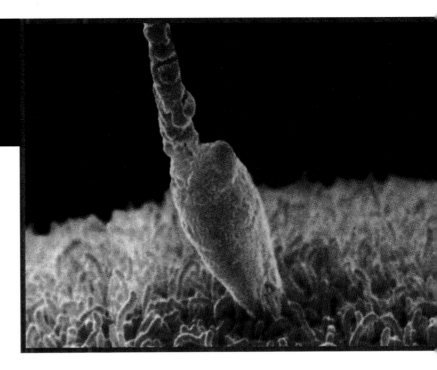

This colored micrograph shows a single sperm fertilizing a human egg. Of the thousands of sperm that made it through the uterus to the egg, only this one will succeed in fertilization.

The sperm must negotiate the **vagina, cervix,** and uterus, where millions become lost or run out of energy. Millions more leave the uterus along the wrong fallopian tube, where there is no egg. Even so, thousands of sperm reach the area around the egg cell.

Meeting of egg and sperm

Of the millions of sperm cells, only one can fertilize the egg cell. The sperm's front end, or nose cap, comes up against an outer protective layer around the egg cell, called the zona pellucida. The sperm uses chemicals called **enzymes** to dissolve its way through this protective layer, and the head of the sperm merges with the outer membrane of the egg cell.

Once this happens, the sperm's single set of **genetic** material, or **DNA,** packaged as 23 **chromosomes,** passes into the egg cell. It takes its place alongside the egg's set of 23 chromosomes. This forms the complete set of genetic material, at total of 46 chromosomes, so that the fertilized egg can begin development. The outer protective layer of the egg then becomes tougher and harder to prevent other from sperm entering.

Timing of fertilization

The egg cell is able to be fertilized for only one or two days after it leaves the ovary. The sperm cells last for two to four days after their release into the female system. These two time periods must coincide for a sperm to fertilize the egg.

Since an egg cell is usually released on or around day 14 of the **menstrual cycle,** the sperm must arrive a few days before, or after, to make fertilization likely. By knowing when this window of opportunity occurs, a couple can increase their chances of **conceiving** a child. They can also use this information to avoid conception by various natural or calendar methods of contraception.

As the **egg cell** and **sperm** cell join at **fertilization**, the **genetic** makeup of the future human body becomes fixed, including whether it is female or male. Now begins the process of **gestation** or pregnancy, which lasts nine months, until the baby is born.

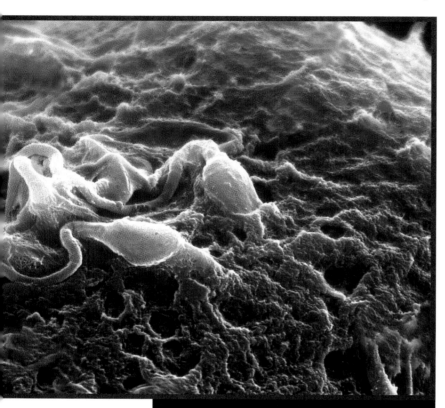

A sperm cell pushes its way through the outer protective layer of the egg cell, so its genetic material can enter the egg.

Early pregnancy

The fertilized egg cell splits into two cells, which each then divide in two, and so on. They increase in numbers by the cell division process of **mitosis**. Each resulting cell receives the full set of genetic information, or **DNA**. The number of cells rises rapidly into the hundreds to form the early **embryo**.

Implantation

A week or so after fertilization, the still-microscopic ball of cells burrows into the soft, blood-rich lining, or **endometrium**, of the **uterus**, which has been prepared by the female cycle. Here, the embryo will be protected and nourished.

An embryo that implants into another area, such as in the **fallopian tube** or even the abdominal cavity, cannot survive. It causes the woman great pain and bleeding and is called an ectopic pregnancy. This is a rare event. Each year only 1 woman in 15,000 requires treatment for an ectopic pregnancy.

Middle weeks

The cells in the embryo continue to divide—into thousands and millions. About two months after fertilization, the embryo is just 0.5 to 0.8 inches (15 to 20 millimeters) long—the size of a small grape. However, many of its main body parts and organs are forming. Both male and female embryos are similar at this stage.

Miscarriage

A miscarriage is when a pregnancy ends early, with the loss of the developing baby. There are various causes, including a malformed embryo or fetus, illness, imbalance of hormones, or reproductive system problems in the mother. A pregnancy ended deliberately by medical means is usually known as a termination, or planned abortion.

The vital stage

From eight weeks after fertilization, the developing baby takes on a recognizable human form and is called a **fetus.** The next two weeks see changes in the internal reproductive parts. In a female fetus, the main reproductive organs become the **ovaries.** In the male, they become the **testes.** Between ten and twelve weeks, differences become obvious from the outside. The **vagina** forms in a female, and the penis grows in a male.

Development problems

During these early stages of reproductive system formation, several rare problems may occur and be present at birth. In some cases these malformations are due to inheritance; that is, they are caused by abnormal genetic material from one or both parents. In others they are caused by damaging chemicals or conditions experienced by the mother. These include various drugs, harmful X-rays or radiation (which is why expectant mothers are rarely given X-rays), and infections such as rubella, or German measles.

Undescended testes

The male embryo's testes develop inside the **abdomen.** About two months before birth, they move, or descend, into the **scrotum.** If they have not descended by birth, this is known as cryptorchism or undescended testes. The descent may still occur naturally, but if delay continues, there is a danger of future fertility problems. Treatment may include surgery or **hormone** therapy.

This ultrasound scan shows an unborn baby looking up to the left. The head is at top right.

CHILDBIRTH

Childbirth occurs when a baby leaves the **uterus**, passes along the birth canal or **vagina**, and enters the outside world. Childbirth usually occurs in three stages.

First stage

The uterus enlarges greatly during pregnancy, and its walls contain some of the body's most powerful muscles. As birth begins, the **hormone** oxytocin from the **pituitary gland** causes the uterine muscles to begin to contract. The muscles squeeze the baby against the tightly closed neck of the uterus, the **cervix**.

Gradually the cervix relaxes and widens, or dilates. The mother feels the muscular contractions with great discomfort or pain. They become more powerful and frequent, one every two or three minutes. This first stage is called labor and lasts, on average, twelve to sixteen hours for the mother's first baby. It is usually not as long for later babies.

At some point, the mother's water "breaks." The fluid that surrounded and cushioned the baby in the uterus, called amniotic fluid, flows out through the cervix and vagina.

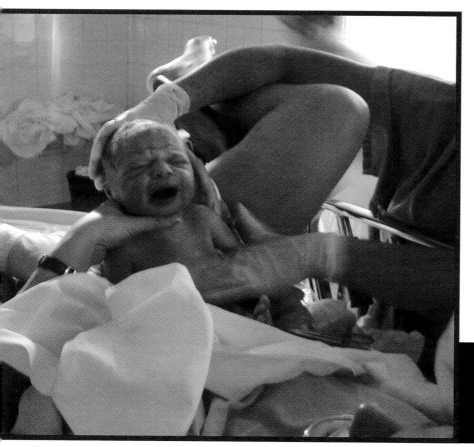

Second stage

Continuing contractions of the uterine muscles push the baby against the cervix, which dilates to about four inches (ten centimeters) across. The baby begins to move and passes through the cervix and along the vagina to the outside. This stage, called delivery, may take a couple of hours or only a few minutes.

Birth is strenuous and tiring for both mother and baby. Both need plenty of rest afterward.

Third stage

In the uterus, **nutrients,** oxygen, and other substances pass from mother to baby through the placenta. The placenta develops in the uterine lining and is attached to the baby by **blood vessels** known as the umbilical cord. When the baby is born, it is still attached to the placenta until the cord is cut. In the third stage, the placenta emerges from the uterus. This usually takes 20 to 30 minutes.

Birth positions

Most babies are born headfirst. The head is the baby's widest part, and its smooth surface eases the journey through the cervix and vagina. However, the baby may be in a different position, such as buttocks first, called breech presentation, or arm or leg first. Attending medical staff may be able to move the baby into the correct position.

Babies born early, or in poor health, are kept warm and germ-free in an incubator.

Assisted birth

The mother can be given pain relief by breathing in a special gas mixture or using various types of painkilling drugs. Epidural anesthesia is the injection of a painkilling drug into the lower back. This blocks feelings of pain from the lower body.

In case of problems, the birth process can be helped in various ways. Episiotomy is a small cut made to widen the vagina so that the baby can pass through without tearing the vagina. Forceps are curved, paddlelike devices that fit around the baby's head. They can be used to change the baby's position or help pull it out. Occasionally a Caesarean section is needed, usually because the baby is in danger. In this operation, the baby is born from the front of the **abdomen,** through a careful incision made in its wall and uterus.

Premature birth

In some cases a baby is premature, or born before its due date. These babies are usually smaller and less developed than those born after a full pregnancy, and they often need special care. They are kept warm in an incubator, given nutrients and fluid through tubes into the body, and perhaps given oxygen through a tube into the lungs. They are also carefully monitored for any signs of illness.

In the **uterus,** the baby receives oxygen from its mother by way of the placenta and umbilical cord. But after birth, the baby usually cries to open its breathing system and take in life-giving oxygen. Then the baby begins to feed on milk, made in the **mammary glands** in the mother's breasts.

Hormones and milk

Two reproductive **hormones,** both from the **pituitary gland,** control the production and release of milk. Prolactin stimulates the mammary glands to produce milk. Oxytocin is released in response to the sensations of the baby suckling. It stimulates the release of milk from the breast through the nipple. This process is known as lactation.

For the first day or two, the baby does not receive regular milk but instead a clearer fluid called colostrum. This is already in the mother's breasts at birth. It is rich in **proteins** and may help strengthen the baby's **immune system** to resist disease. It also encourages the baby's **digestive system** to begin working regularly. Colostrum is replaced after a couple of days with normal milk.

Weaning

As a baby grows bigger and stronger, the **nutrients** its body needs change. Gradually mother's milk becomes less suitable, and the baby starts to eat solid or normal foods. The time when a baby stops feeding on mother's milk is known as weaning. It is often linked more to social tradition and family lifestyle than to the baby's nutritional needs.

A small system

The reproductive system is the only main body system that is not working at birth. In fact, it is not yet fully formed. All of its parts are present, but most are relatively small compared to the overall size of the body and its other systems. The reproductive system grows with

Childhood changes

Normally the reproductive organs change little during childhood. Rarely in a young girl there may be discharge from the **vagina.** This is generally no cause for concern but should be reported to her doctor. In a young boy, the penis may occasionally become stiffer, or erect. This is fairly normal, but if it becomes common and frequent, it too should be reported to a doctor. Any signs of redness, swelling, irritation, or lumps should receive medical attention.

the rest of the body during childhood but stays relatively small and nonfunctioning. There is little obvious outward difference between girls and boys in terms of overall body size and shape.

From seven or eight years of age, on average, production of reproductive hormones begins to rise slightly. In girls this is the female sex hormone **estrogen** from the **ovaries.** In a boy they are androgens, chiefly the male sex hormone **testosterone,** from the **testes.** However, the amounts of these hormones are not sufficient to cause any bodily changes until about ten years of age in girls and twelve years in boys. This marks the early stage of **puberty.**

During childhood, girls and boys are physically similar in overall size and shape.

ADOLESCENCE AND PUBERTY

Adolescence is usually described as the stage between childhood and adulthood. It varies hugely among different societies and traditions. In some cases it lasts several years, typically the teenage years, and has its own conventions, customs, fashions, and lifestyle. In other cases it occurs over a short time, when a "rite of passage" event marks the rapid change from girl to woman or boy to man.

The teenage years may be a time of worry and anxiety, but it is also an exciting period of rapid physical change and increasing social freedom.

A time of change

During adolescence, many changes in the reproductive system occur, as it grows and becomes mature or able to produce children. This time of bodily change and sexual development is known as **puberty.**

Girls experience puberty at a slightly younger age than boys, and the events occur closer together over a shorter time. The average age of puberty in Western societies is about twelve years for girls and fourteen for males. On average, it lasts two to three years for girls and four years for boys. However, there is great variation. This is partly due to inherited factors. If a mother went through puberty early, her daughter is likely to, as well.

Worries about puberty

There is considerable variation in the timing of puberty. Some female changes begin at nine years of age, while some male changes are still occurring at eighteen. Early or late puberty, including delayed menarche, may cause worry and distress. But in the majority of cases, there is no cause for concern. A medical checkup can provide reassurance.

Female changes

Development of the female body at puberty is due to increasing levels of estrogen, the female **hormone** produced by the **ovaries.** It has many effects:

- The whole body grows much more rapidly, especially in height.
- The breasts enlarge, and the nipples become more prominent.
- Body hair appears, most prominently under the arms and between the legs.
- The main reproductive organs enlarge, and hormonal changes begin the **menstrual cycle.**
- The first menstrual cycle is known as **menarche.** It usually occurs when a girl's weight reaches 99 to 106 pounds (45 to 48 kilograms) rather than a certain height or age. The first several cycles may not involve the release of an **egg cell.**
- Body proportions change, the hips widen, and the body outline becomes more curved.

Male changes

Development of the male body at puberty is due to increasing levels of male hormones, especially **testosterone,** produced by the **testes.** The effects include the following:

- The body grows much more rapidly, especially in height.
- Body hair appears, most prominently on the face, under the arms, and between the legs.
- The main reproductive organs enlarge—most noticeably the testes and penis.
- The voice "breaks" or "cracks" and becomes deeper.
- Body proportions change. The shoulders broaden, and the body outline becomes more angular.

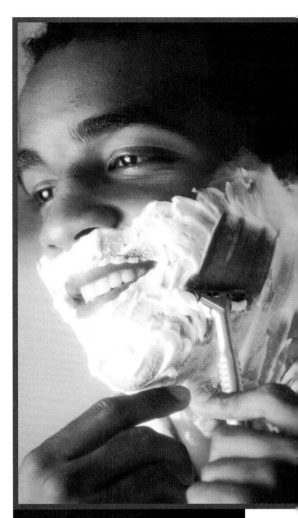

Young males usually begin shaving during puberty, as the amount of facial hair increases.

Varicocele

Varicocele tends to occur in adolescent males. It is due to distended or varicose veins in the testis. It may cause a swelling around the testis and a dragging ache. Initial treatment involves wearing an athletic support. The problem may clear on its own or with a small operation.

FERTILITY PROBLEMS

Difficulty in **conceiving** a baby is usually called low fertility, while inability to conceive is known as infertility. However, the process of reproduction is long and complex and, to some extent, subject to chance. Often, couples who doubted they would ever have a child are suddenly surprised to find they are expecting a new baby.

It takes two

A fertility problem may be based in the male reproductive system, the female reproductive system, or a combination of the two. The inability to conceive is usually regarded first as a problem of both partners, until examinations and tests reveal the exact cause.

Lack of fertility may simply be due to lack of understanding about the reproductive process. For example, the **egg cell** can be **fertilized** only during a short part of the **menstrual cycle,** just after the ovary releases the egg. Attempts to conceive should be made around this time.

Male problems

A healthy male releases some 300 to 500 million active **sperm** during ejaculation. It seems to be important that many survive the journey to approach the egg, as together they produce a substance called acrosin, which allows one of them to fertilize the egg. Having a low sperm count may cause reduced fertility, as can sperm that are malformed or do not swim actively. Sperm are produced continuously by the male reproductive system. However, their numbers may fall due to a problem in the system, such as low **testosterone** production, infection, or a growth. Or the cause may be elsewhere in the body. For example, the man may have a general infection or disease. Fatigue, stress, or various medications can also affect sperm.

Low sperm count is a rare side effect of certain drugs and other treatments. Also, the production of sperm naturally reduces with age, from about 50 to 60 years, although it can be retained past the age of 75. Problems that interfere with **sexual intercourse** and the release of sperm also affect fertility.

Female problems

Many conditions can affect the balance of **hormones** controlling the menstrual cycle. As in the male, these include conditions elsewhere in the body, such as a general infection or disease, the effects of fatigue, stress, severe emotions, or certain medications. Problems in the brain or **pituitary gland** also affect fertility, since the pituitary is in charge of the hormonal system, including the reproductive hormones.

Stress can cause fertility problems for both males and females.

As described earlier, various infections and inflammations can affect the female reproductive system. For example, infection of the **fallopian tubes** may cause scarring that blocks the tubes, preventing ripe eggs from passing to the **uterus.**

Various fluids and secretions line the passages of the female reproductive system. In some cases the balance of chemicals can damage the sperm or the sticky mucus of the **cervix** lining may be too thick for the sperm to get through.

Keeping cool

Sperm are produced most effectively at 95 to 96.8°F (35 to 36°C), slightly lower than normal body temperature. The position of the **testes** in the **scrotum,** below the body, maintains this cooler temperature. Factors that increase testis temperature, such as fever or wearing tight undergarments, can reduce sperm production and affect fertility.

FERTILITY CONTROL

It is not always desirable for **sexual intercourse** to result in a baby. Methods to prevent this are known as fertility control, birth control, or contraception. Each method has advantages and disadvantages in effectiveness, ease of use, side effects, convenience, and personal preference. For example, the contraceptive pill must be taken at the advised intervals, or it may become much less effective. Also, social customs, traditions, and religious beliefs affect the choice of method or even if one is permitted. Some people choose the single most certain method of contraception—abstaining from sexual intercourse.

IUD

An intrauterine device (IUD) is fitted into the **uterus.** It alters conditions slightly so that the **embryo** cannot implant into the uterine lining. There are different shapes and designs of IUDs, such as the loop and coil.

Barrier methods

The condom is a flexible rubber bag that fits firmly over the penis. It traps the **sperm** as they are released, so they cannot enter the female system. The cervical cap and diaphragm are barrier devices that fit firmly over the **cervix.** They prevent sperm from entering the uterus.

Sponges and chemicals

The foam sponge is inserted into the **vagina** and contains spermicide, or sperm-killing chemicals. Foams and jellies are available for the same task. They are used just before sexual intercourse, usually combined with other methods, such as a condom.

Pills

Birth control pills are also called oral contraceptives. They contain **hormones** that alter the **menstrual cycle.** There are two main types

Uses and risks of the "pill"
Birth control pills can be used to ease heavy periods and pain, and they may protect against ovarian cysts, anemia, rheumatoid arthritis, breast lumps, and certain infections. However, research has also linked pill use with cancers of the breast and cervix, high blood pressure, blood clots, and other problems. Taken with medical approval and regular checkups, most pills are extremely safe.

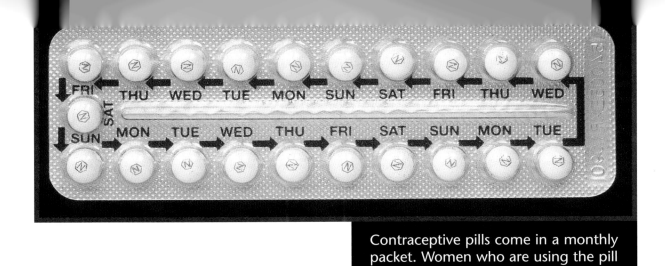

Contraceptive pills come in a monthly packet. Women who are using the pill must remember to take one each day.

of pills. The standard or combined pill contains **estrogen** and **progesterone**. They trick the **pituitary gland** into altering the menstrual cycle. The result is that the **ovaries** do not release ripe **eggs,** and the lining of the uterus alters so it cannot receive an early embryo. The progesterone-only or minipill is more suited to women who could be at risk of conditions such as high blood pressure or blood clots.

Timing (calendar or rhythm) methods

Conception can occur only during a few days of the menstrual cycle. The calendar or rhythm method is based on avoiding sexual intercourse during this time. Two techniques make this method more accurate. One is measuring the small rise in body temperature (about half a degree) that occurs just after the egg is released. The other is checking the mucus produced by the cervix, which becomes thinner and clearer a few days before the egg is released.

Surgical methods

Sterilization is a surgical procedure carried out as a permanent form of birth control. In tubal ligation, the **fallopian tubes** are tied or cut, so egg **cells** cannot travel from the ovary to the uterus. In a vasectomy, the **vas deferens** are tied or cut, so sperm cannot leave the **testes** and **epididymides.** These methods are regarded as nonreversible.

How effective?

On average, with correct use, the different methods of contraception are listed from most to least effective:
- abstinence
- contraceptive pill
- IUD
- condom plus spermicide
- diaphragm plus spermicide
- diaphragm
- timing (calendar or rhythm) methods
- spermicide alone.

Only abstinence and condoms provide protection against STDs.

ASSISTED REPRODUCTION

Recent years have seen great advances in reproductive medicine. Whole new areas of expertise have grown in the areas of reproduction and **genetics**, based largely on continually improving technology and drugs.

However, the function of the reproductive system is making babies, and babies occupy the emotions, hearts, and minds of many people. Birth is also one of the few bodily events subject to laws and regulations. It is not surprising that reproductive medicine generates much discussion.

A slight change in body temperature occurs around ovulation.

Fertility drugs

Several **hormone**-containing medications stimulate the ripening and release of **egg cells**. These are used when the **menstrual cycle** is erratic or irregular. However, such medications can have various side effects, including the release of several eggs at **ovulation**, which can result in a multiple pregnancy.

Surgical methods

Advanced surgical methods can now correct structural problems of the reproductive system, which were almost untreatable several years ago. Microsurgical equipment and techniques can remove blockages or correct malformations, for example, in the **fallopian tubes** or **vas deferens**.

IVF

Normal **fertilization** takes place in the fallopian tube of the female reproductive system. IVF, in vitro fertilization, is when egg and **sperm** are joined outside the body, usually in laboratory equipment. (*In vitro* means "in glass.") The term "test-tube baby" is sometimes used to describes babies **conceived** this way, although fertilization is more likely to take place in a flat, round petri dish than in a test tube.

There are many forms of IVF. In the basic method, ripe egg cells are removed from the woman's **ovary** through a small incision in the **abdomen**. They are then added to sperm cells in a laboratory container of warm **nutrient** liquid. An egg cell that is fertilized undergoes very early stages of **embryo** formation. It can be identified

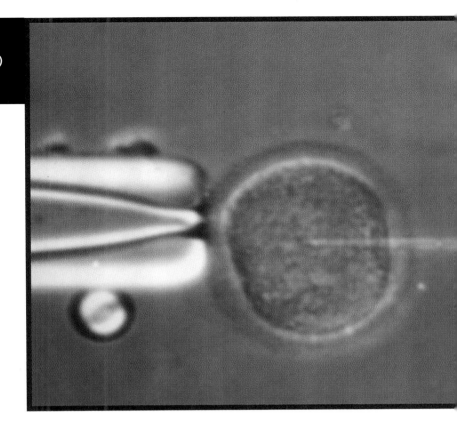

An egg cell is held gently on the end of a pipette (tiny pipe) ready for IVF.

under a microscope and then inserted into the woman's **uterus** through the **vagina** to continue normal development.

Other methods of IVF include bringing the sperm and egg together in the fallopian tube or replacing the fertilized egg there. The success rate of these procedures is steadily increasing.

Donors and surrogacy

In some cases a man cannot produce sperm cells, or a woman is unable to produce egg cells. Sperm or eggs may then be used from another person— a donor.

In other cases, a woman can produce eggs, but she is unable to become pregnant, perhaps because of uterine or hormonal problems. Following IVF, using her egg cell and her partner's sperm, the embryo may be inserted into the uterus of another woman, known as a surrogate mother. The baby is genetically the child of the couple, although it is born to the surrogate mother.

Controversies

Advances in reproductive medicine generate much controversy. Background research into assisted reproduction involves the use of eggs, sperm, and embryos. Should embryos be used and then destroyed in this way? Should a baby have its genetic material changed by **gene therapy**?

The speed of medical progress has left many people undecided about social and moral issues. This is reflected in official guidelines and regulations, which vary greatly from nation to nation. What is permitted in one country may be illegal in another.

Reproduction relies on **genetics**. The **egg cell** and **sperm** cell each contain a set of human genetic material. These contribute equally to the genetic makeup of the new individual. **Genes** contain the basic instructions for life, development, and growth of the human body—including its reproductive system.

Reproduction and chromosomes

Human genetic material comes in the form of 46 **chromosomes** containing **DNA**. The chromosomes occur in 23 pairs. One of each pair came from the mother by way of the egg cell, and one of each pair came from the father by way of the sperm cell. Of the 23 pairs, 22 are always very similar. In a female the two chromosomes of the 23rd pair are also very similar in size and shape. Both are known as X. In a male the 23rd pair differ. One is X. The other is smaller, has a different shape, and is known as Y. X and Y are called sex chromosomes.

Male or female?

When sperm or eggs form in the reproductive system, they contain only one chromosome from each pair, including the 23rd pair. So every egg cell contains one X. In the male system, there is an equal chance that either an X or a Y from the 23rd pair will pass into a sperm. So some sperm have an X, while others have a Y. If an X-carrying sperm fertilizes the egg, the X chromosome will pair with the X in the egg, and the result is XX, a girl. If a Y-carrying sperm fertilizes the egg, the resulting pair will be XY, producing a boy.

IVF has helped many couples to successfully conceive. But it can be a long and stressful process, requiring several treatments and a lot of professional advice.

The male factor

The differences between X and Y chromosomes are very important. Some serious inherited diseases occur only or mainly in males due to problems on the Y chromosome. One such problem is hemophilia, where the blood does not clot properly to seal a wound.

Advances

In advancing techniques such as IVF, early **embryos** outside the body can be tested to determine whether they are male or female. They can also be tested for the presence of certain genes that may carry inherited conditions. This might allow parents to select which embryo should continue development.

Whatever scientific advances occur in the future, reproduction will remain the most important and amazing natural process of the body. Without it, there would be no families—and no more people.

Techniques to manipulate the workings of the human reproductive system, genes, and the entire reproductive process are progressing rapidly. The future carries hope for some, such as couples wishing to have healthy children, but great worries for others.

Reproduction and life

Reproduction is a central feature of life itself. Yet for an individual person, the parts of the reproductive system are not essential for basic survival. A human body can exist without some or most of them.

However, for many people, having babies, raising children, and being part of a family are central to life's experiences. These activities bring pleasure and joy as well as worry and heartache. It is the product of the reproductive system—when parents have offspring—rather than the system itself that makes it so important in our lives.

WHAT CAN GO WRONG WITH MY REPRODUCTIVE SYSTEM?

The table below summarizes some of the problems that can affect the reproductive system. It also gives information about how each problem is treated.

Many problems can be avoided by healthy behaviors. This is called prevention. Getting regular exercise and plenty of rest are important, as is eating a balanced diet. The table below offers some of the ways you can prevent injury and illness.

Remember, if you think something is wrong with your body, talk to a trained medical professional, such as a doctor or school nurse. Regular checkups are an important part of maintaining a healthy body.

Illness or injury	Cause	Symptoms	Prevention	Treatment
PMS (Pre-menstrual syndrome)	Changing balance of hormones and other chemicals in the body a few days before the period starts; perhaps diet and general health.	Changes in mood, feelings, and emotions; body changes such as bloated feeling in the stomach.	Difficult to prevent; perhaps changes in lifestyle, including more exercise, a balanced diet, and stopping smoking.	Lifestyle changes; in severe cases, where PMS interferes with home, school, or work, drugs may be prescribed.
Endometriosis	Pieces of the uterine lining end up in the lower body cavity.	Dragging pains and extra amounts of normal period bleeding.	None.	**Hormone** therapy and perhaps surgery.
Low sperm count	Failure of the **testes** to develop properly; diseases such as mumps; overheating in the **scrotum**.	Inability to **conceive.**	Mumps can be prevented by vaccination; wearing loose undergarments may help.	Infertility can be treated with artificial methods of conception.

Illness or injury	Cause	Symptoms	Prevention	Treatment
STDs	Various **microbes** transmitted by sexual contact.	Discharge, inflammation, itching, pain in genital area.	Practicing safe sex; limiting the number of sexual partners; good personal hygiene.	Depends on exact cause, but usually drug therapy.
Cervical cancer	Not clear. Cancer is caused by a variety of substances. Some people may be more likely to develop cancer than others.	Abnormal **vaginal** discharge and bleeding, pain, and general ill health.	Not yet clear. Regular pap smear tests can detect the disease at an early stage, when it is much easier to treat.	A combination of drugs, radiation, and surgery.
Ovarian cyst	Not clear. May result from abnormal ripening of an **egg.**	Pain; pressure on **bladder**; menstrual changes.	Not clear.	If cancerous, surgery, radiation, and drugs.
BPH, enlarged prostate	Not clear.	Interferes with urination.	Not clear.	Drugs and surgery.
HIV/AIDS	The HIV **virus.**	Initial symptoms include fever, sore throat, and swollen glands. Symptoms can then disappear for years. Then the body's **immune system** fails.	Practicing safe sex and using a condom substantially lessen the risk, as does not sharing hypodermic needles.	There is no cure. Drugs are available that can delay the onset.
Testicular cancer	Not clear.	Trouble urinating; lump in the testis.	Not clear, but regular self-exams is vital to early detection and successful treatment.	Surgery, radiation, and drugs.

Further reading

Connolly, Sean. *STDs*. Chicago: Heinemann Library, 2002.

Nolan, Mary. *Teen Pregnancy*. Chicago: Heinemann Library, 2002.

O'Donnell, Kerri. *The Reproductive System*. New York: The Rosen Publishing Group, Inc., 2000.

Snedden, Robert. *Cell Division & Genetics*. Chicago: Heinemann Library, 2003.

GLOSSARY

abdomen lower part of the torso, between the chest and hips

adolescence time when a child grows rapidly and matures into an adult, physically and mentally

antibiotic drug used to destroy harmful bacteria and fungi

bacterium (plural is **bacteria**) microorganism that can cause disease

bladder baglike organ in the lower abdomen that stores urine

blood vessel tube that carries blood around the body

cell microscopic unit or building block of a living thing. The body is made of billions of cells.

cervix main opening at the base of the uterus. It opens into the vagina.

chromosome threadlike structure in a cell, containing the genetic material, or DNA

conceive to create a new life when an egg joins a sperm at fertilization

digestive system system in the body that takes in, breaks down, and absorbs foods

DNA (deoxyribonucleic acid) the substance that carries genetic instructions, or genes

egg egg cell or ovum; the female reproductive cell

embryo early stage in the development of a living thing. In humans this stage lasts for eight weeks after fertilization.

endometrium inner, blood-rich lining of the uterus

enzyme protein that helps chemical reactions occur

epididymis coiled tube next to the testis that stores sperm as they mature

estrogen female hormone that controls the menstrual cycle and sexual development

fallopian tube tube that leads from the ovary to the uterus

fertilization joining of an egg cell and a sperm cell, along with their genetic material

fetus stage in the development of a living thing. This stage occurs after the embryo but before birth.

follicle tiny sac-like body part where eggs ripen

gene instruction for life that exists as genetic material, or DNA

genetic having to do with genes

gene therapy treatment to cure genetic diseases by introducing normal genes

gestation pregnancy; the time when a baby develops within its mother before birth

hormone chemical made in the body that travels around the body and affects organs and tissues in a variety of ways

immune system system that defends the body against infection

ligament strong band of fibers that holds a joint together

mammary gland one of two female parts specialized to produce milk for a baby

meiosis type of cell division that produces four cells from one, with each resulting cell having half the normal set of genetic material

menarche time of the first menstrual cycle

menopause stage of life when the menstrual cycle ceases

menstrual cycle sequence of events in which an egg ripens and the female body becomes ready to nourish an embryo

microbe very small living thing visible only under a microscope

mitosis type of cell division that produces two cells from one, with each resulting cell having the complete normal set of genetic material

nucleus central part of a cell that contains the genetic material, or DNA

nutrient part of food that the body can use

ovary main female reproductive part, which produces ripe eggs and the hormone estrogen

ovulation release of a ripe egg from the ovary

ovum egg cell or egg; the female reproductive cell

peristalsis wavelike muscle contractions that help push or massage substances along

pituitary gland important hormone-producing gland located just below the brain

protein type of large molecule that makes up some of the basic structures of all living things

puberty sexual development from child to mature adult

scrotum bag or sac that contains the two main male parts, the testes

seminal vesicle small male body part that produces fluid to contain sperm cells

sexual intercourse activity involving contact of the genitals, usually with the penis inserted into the vagina

sperm the male reproductive cell

testis main male reproductive part, which produces sperm and the hormone testosterone

testosterone male hormone that controls sperm production and a boy's sexual development

uterus part of the a woman's reproductive system where a baby develops before birth

vagina part of the birth canal, linking the uterus with the outside

vas deferens tube that carries the sperm from the testis and epididymis on their journey from the body

virus very small microorganism that can cause infection

INDEX